SUBMERGED

THIRTY DAYS OF DROPPING INTO THE
HEART OF GOD

SHAWN W. THOMPSON

SPIRIT-LED
PUBLISHING

shawnwthompson@icloud.com

Unless otherwise indicated, all Scripture quotations are from the ESV® Bible (The Holy Bible, English Standard Version®), copyright © 2001 by Crossway, a publishing ministry of Good News Publishers. Used by permission. All rights reserved.

Scripture quotations marked (NLT) are taken from the Holy Bible, New Living Translation, copyright © 1996, 2004, 2007 by Tyndale House Foundation. Used by permission of Tyndale House Publishers, Inc., Carol Stream, Illinois 60188. All rights reserved.

Scripture quotations marked (NET) are taken from the NET Bible® copyright ©1996-2016 by Biblical Studies Press, L.L.C. All rights reserved."

Editing: Sally Hanan of Inksnatcher.com
Book Layout: BookDesignTemplates.com
Cover Design: Alexa Lasco

Ordering Information:
Quantity sales. Special discounts are available on quantity purchases by corporations, associations, and others. For details, contact the author at the e-mail address above.

Submerged / Shawn Thompson
ISBN 978-1-943011-96-4

I wish to thank God, the Father, for giving us the gift of the Spirit. Through this relationship, we are given direct relationship to the one who is love. It is because of this unmerited relationship with him that we have direct access to the Father's heart.

I would also like to thank my dearly loved friends John and Amy Meyer for always encouraging me in the love of the Father. And last, but by no means least, I would like to thank my dear mother for always unconditionally loving and supporting me.

PROLOGUE

My intention for writing this book is to share with you, the reader, what I believe and have experienced the heart of God to be like. I hope that after reading it, you will have an increase in faith, favor, and a clear vision of who you really are; that you would truly see yourself through the eyes of heaven and fully put on the new man, who is in Jesus. I believe that when we break the chains of shame, guilt, and condemnation, we begin to understand God's true heart. His heart is to love us unconditionally, no matter the circumstances, and he wants us to truly be able to understand that upon believing in Jesus, we fully put on the righteousness that is in Christ. God no longer has expectations of us merely to perform good deeds; rather, we are to love as Christ did. After all, Jesus did not die on the cross so we could have a religion called Christianity. I don't believe this to be the case at all. Christ died so we could become a new creation in him, so that his Spirit could come and fall on us, causing us to love one another with fervent, unconditional, undying love. The result of this is to experience a true freedom: freedom from striving to achieve goals or always trying to be "good enough" to please God. I am, myself, a refugee of "religion." I don't believe Jesus came and died for us so we could go back to performing religion the way the Pharisees and Sadducees did. We are born again, new in Christ to experience freedom and life more abundantly. So come, church, enjoy freedom and love the way God intended. I hope this next thirty days will be uplifting and help lead you to true freedom in Christ.

Mahalo,

Shawn Thompson

DAY 1

GENESIS 1:1–2

In the beginning, God created the heavens and the earth. The earth was without form and void, and darkness was over the face of the deep. And the Spirit of God was hovering over the face of the waters.

INSIGHT

To better understand the vastness of God and his love for us, we look to Genesis. Within mere seconds of opening our Bibles, God shows us he is the one who created heaven and earth, and that he has always had community with the Spirit, thus laying out the foundation for the Trinity. What is truly amazing to me is that the same God of Genesis is the same God who counts every hair on our heads (Luke 12:7).

PRAYER

Father in heaven, glorious is your name and wondrous is your love. What adoration I have for you, God. You created the heavens and the earth, yet you care to know my name. Thank you, God, for creating me to be unique, and for giving me your Spirit. Let me not forget this day, nor how vast your love is for me. Cause me to be in constant awe of your creation. May all of my focus be on you, Lord, for you are the God who has existed since before the foundation of the earth. I pray, God, that each day I live out on your earth be a reminder of your love. I pray that each day I would get to soak up your beautiful creation and make your glory known. Help me to fathom how a God so big is still such a personal God. Thank you, Lord. May glory be to you forever and ever, amen.

DAY 2

JOHN 1:1–5 (NLT)

In the beginning the Word already existed. The Word was with God, and the Word was God. He existed in the beginning with God. God created everything through him, and nothing was created except through him. The Word gave life to everything that was created, and his life brought light to everyone. The light shines in the darkness, and the darkness can never extinguish it.

INSIGHT

Again, we see here that since the beginning, God has always been a God of fellowship. We see community with the Spirit and the Word. It is important to note here that God created everything through the Word, and the Word gave life. The significance of this is realized about ten verses later in John, where we find that the Word become flesh. The Word is Jesus (John 1:14). Jesus gave life in the beginning and continues to give life now. He is the light of the world!

PRAYER

Thank you, Lord, that you are a God of fellowship, and that you have been since the beginning of time. Thank you that despite your vastness, you still desire a relationship with me. I thank you, Papa, for giving me the Advocate, Jesus. He is the one who lights my path. Jesus, I thank you that I have a personal relationship with you, and as I seek you, there is no darkness you cannot cast out! You are my loving God, and I thank you forever and ever, amen.

DAY 3

MATTHEW 3:16–17

And when Jesus was baptized, immediately he went up from the water, and behold, the heavens were opened to him, and he saw the Spirit of God descending like a dove and coming to rest on him; and behold, a voice from heaven said, "This is my beloved Son, with whom I am well pleased."

INSIGHT

The first thing I can't help but notice in these two verses is the humble example Jesus set for us. He, being the Son of God, came to a man to be baptized. John even said, "I need to be baptized by you, and do you come to me?" (v. 14). He said, "He who is coming after me is mightier than I, whose sandals I am not worthy to carry" (v. 11). Jesus humbled himself and received his baptism from John. At that very moment, the Spirit of God fell onto Jesus, and a voice from heaven called Jesus "Son." The amazing truth about this is that we have been given the same Spirit and the same adoption into the family of God.

PRAYER

Lord, thank you for being a humble and loving God. Because of your meekness, I am able to receive the Spirit and be adopted into your heavenly family. Thank you, God, for being a humble example to me. Cause me, Lord, to live as you did, and to be humble, each day exalting you in every moment. Thank you again, Lord, for my unmerited adoption into your heavenly family. Thank you that the same Spirit you gave Jesus is the same Spirit you gave me. Each day the Spirit cries out on my behalf *Abba Father.* That is true; I am one of your sons and daughters. To you be the glory forever and ever, amen.

DAY 4

JOHN 14:6–7

Jesus said to him, "I am the way, and the truth, and the life. No one comes to the Father except through me. If you had known me, you would have known my Father also. From now on you do know him and have seen him."

INSIGHT

Here we see how confident Jesus was in his heavenly position; he knew he was the Son of God. He was not being boastful. He was just saying how it was. Jesus was humble and meek. His character did not shrink away from his knowledge of who God said he was. He said, "No one can come to the Father except through me." He was speaking into both the present and the future—when Jesus would ascend and the Spirit would come to dwell in the body of Christ. He again was showing his relationship in the Trinity, one he had had since the beginning.

PRAYER

Lord, I come to you as your humble servant. I
thank you that you have placed in me a vision of
who I am from heaven's perspective. I pray,
Father, that I would not shrink away from who
you say I am, but that I would embrace my
heavenly reflection. Even if I am called to do great
things, I know that it is you who does the work in
me. I no longer strive for perfection but am found
perfect in your sight, thanks to the great love you
have shown me. Thank you, Jesus, for becoming
the mediator to my heavenly Father, and that I
have a direct and personal relationship with him
because of you. May the peace and glory of your
magnificent love rest on me forever and ever,
amen.

DAY 5

JOHN 19:28–30

Jesus knew that his mission was now finished, and to fulfil Scripture he said, "I am thirsty." A jar of sour wine was sitting there, so they soaked a sponge in it, put it on a hyssop branch, and held it up to his lips. When Jesus had tasted it, he said, "It is finished!" Then he bowed his head and released his spirit.

INSIGHT

Jesus was not only totally engulfed by the Spirit, he was also very thorough in his knowledge of the written Word. He often either quoted Scripture or fulfilled prophecy about himself, because he knew he was the written Word. The Word became flesh to walk among us. After he was given the sour wine on the cross, he knew it fulfilled another prophecy. He said, "It is finished." I truly believe these to be the most incredible three words in the entire Bible, because it was at this moment Christ put an end to sin and reconciled the world to God the Father. Our thirst is quenched and Christ has become our spotless lamb.

PRAYER

Lord, I pray that you would make me a person who thirsts for your Word. I pray that it gives me a foundation to stand on. I thank you that I can feast on your Word, and that it satisfies my deep hunger. I thank you, Jesus, for your death on the cross, and that you paid for my sin. I thank you, Lord, that your mercy is new each day, and that I do not have to be a slave to sin. I can rather put on your righteousness. I pray, Lord, that all striving would cease. I will rest in your presence. May all the glory be to you forever and ever, amen.

DAY 6

COLOSSIANS 1:20–22 (NLT)

And through him God reconciled everything to himself ... by means of Christ's blood on the cross. This includes you who ... were his enemies, separated from him by your evil thoughts and actions. Yet now he has ... brought you into his own presence, and you are holy and blameless as you stand before him without a single fault.

INSIGHT

God reconciled heaven, earth, and everything in it through the cross! Now we can really understand how Jesus was able to say "It is finished" with such boldness while dying on the cross. Why, then, do we doubt our heavenly reflection of righteousness? Is it that the original sin of Adam is greater than Jesus's work on the cross? Why is it we can believe so easily that sin came to the world through one man, Adam, but we are always stumbling over the truth that through one man, Jesus, sin is taken away? Can't we be a people satisfied by his sacrifice, which has given us peace and joy in him?

PRAYER

Lord, I pray I would be a person who completely
stands on the finished work of Jesus, and that I
would stop looking to my own deeds for validation
of my righteousness. Let it be your lovingkindness
that leads me to repentance, Lord. Break down my
thinking that it's my repentance that leads to your
lovingkindness. I know that's not your heart. I
know it's you that first loved me. I know you have
called me to love others in the same way. Let love
be my motive to serve you. Let love be my reason
to serve others. Let your love dwell in me.
Through your Spirit, you make me perfect and
blameless in your sight. You are my God, now let
me show the world your truth through your love.
May the glory be to you, my Father in heaven,
forever and ever, amen.

DAY 7

ROMANS 4:4–8

Now to the one who works, his wages are not counted as a gift but as his due. And to the one who does not work but believes in him who justifies the ungodly, his faith is counted as righteousness ... "Blessed are those whose lawless deeds are forgiven, and whose sins are covered; blessed is the man against whom the Lord will not count his sin."

INSIGHT

Here we can see a good contrast between faith and works. The Bible never says that works are bad, just that works are not how we attain righteousness. It is always through faith that we attain righteousness. All work should be a derivative of first having faith! The completed, perfect work of Jesus now grants us perfect peace with God by faith in him. It is a free gift to us so we can be finished with striving to be good enough for God and simply live for his glory. We do not have to work for righteousness, but only seek him who gives life.

PRAYER

Oh, Jesus, thank you tremendously for your finished work on the cross. Thank you that I am able to truly cease from striving and can let go of all my heavy burdens. I can let go of everything in my life that does not reflect the character of Jesus. May my work be a response to my faith in you. May you guide me into your perfect will for my life. I hold firm in the confidence of your promises. I trust in you, God, and today I am letting go! Today I am putting aside the old to put on the new! Today I see myself in your heavenly reflection! May I be a person who never looks back, but is always in pursuit of your presence. To you be the glory forever and ever, amen.

DAY 8

1 PETER 1:10–12

This salvation was something even the prophets wanted to know more about ... They wondered what time or situation the Spirit of Christ within them was talking about when he told them in advance about Christ's suffering and his great glory afterward. They were told that their messages were not for themselves, but for you. And now this Good News has been announced to you by those who preached in the power of the Holy Spirit sent from heaven. It is all so wonderful that even the angels are eagerly watching these things happen.

INSIGHT

Christ said it was better for him to go so that we could have a better advocate, the Spirit. These Old Testament prophets and the angels were not highlighting Christ's life on earth, over the importance of the Spirit, and the free gift of salvation we have in Christ's death on the cross for us. I absolutely love that the angels were eager to see these things fulfilled.

Prayer

Thank you, Lord, for giving me the Spirit. Thank you that the Spirit is such a wonderful gift to me, and that the prophets were searching for the time he would come. The angels were even eagerly waiting on his coming and subsequent glory. Lord, help me to never take the Spirit for granted, but let me cease striving during every moment I get to spend in your presence. I pray I would be able to understand how great a gift the Spirit is, in the same way the angels and prophets did. I thank you for the gift of salvation that is fully based on works, but not my own. Jesus has finished the work, and as a result I enjoy living life in your Spirit. Increase in me today the abundance of your Spirit and the outflowing of your love. To you be the glory forever and ever, amen.

DAY 9

JOHN 13:34–35

A new commandment I give to you, that you love one another: just as I have loved you, you also are to love one another. By this all people will know that you are my disciples, if you have love for one another.

INSIGHT

Sometimes we Christians get really caught up in being "religious," but Jesus brought a new command: to love one another as he loved us. In order to really grasp what this means, we must let go of all preconceptions of "good deeds." We can try to be as good as we want, but aside from Christ and his true love, all of our deeds are as filthy rags. We have been given the ability to live our lives with a Christlike love through the indwelling of the Spirit. It is not that we are so good; it is that he is.

PRAYER

Father, I thank you for your goodness. You are the reason I can know how to truly love. You have set the example of love for me, and you have given me the Advocate who guides my heart in love. I pray today, Father, that I would stop striving to be good, because it's your Spirit living inside me that causes my goodness. I pray, Lord, that you would empty me and prepare me to be filled with the Spirit. I pray I would be a person sensitive to your Spirit, always walking hand in hand with Papa— because it's your Spirit living in me that cries out *Abba Father.* Cause my inner being to fully comprehend my adoption as one of your sons and daughters, to understand that I am no longer a child of this world but a new creation totally overwhelmed by your love. Let my love be perfected in you, God, so I would truly love others as you've loved me. Let me be as part of an orchestra of angels singing praises to heaven. Thank you, Lord, that you are perfecting love in me now. I am letting go, Lord, surrendering to your will and not my own. To you be the glory forever and ever, amen.

DAY 10

MATTHEW 18:1–4

Calling to him a child, he put him in the midst of them and said, "Truly, I say to you, unless you turn and become like children, you will never enter the kingdom of heaven. Whoever humbles himself like this child is the greatest in the kingdom of heaven."

INSIGHT

Jesus, as he often does, was giving us a future tense word. Even though the disciples didn't know yet, I believe Jesus was not only referring to being childlike in an earthly sense, but speaking about our becoming his actual sons and daughters through his future death and resurrection. The totality of this truth is just that much better, for if we really are his sons and daughters, why wouldn't we be childlike? God wants to love on us and guide our lives. Any good father desires the best for his children. It is so important for us to let go and just let God be a papa to us. We have the most loving and personal papa in the world. We just have to let him be Dad.

PRAYER

Papa, I pray today you would hold me in your presence, that I could physically feel you hugging and loving on me. I pray today the realization of my heavenly position in your family would be made known to my heart. Show me that I really am your child, whom you dearly love. Cause me to hold my hands up to you, the way children do when they are tired of walking, because I know many have grown tired. I've been walking on my own for too long. Now my hands are reaching up to you. I ask you to pick me up and carry me. Walk me through life as the Father you are. Make your love for me be the cause of my love and adoration toward you. May you know how much I love my Daddy, and may you lavish your lovingkindness back on me. Help me to truly understand there is no better dad than you, that you are the love of my life. I honor, and praise you forever and ever, amen.

DAY 11

JOHN 15:15 (NET)

I am the true vine and my Father is the gardener. He takes away every branch that does not bear fruit in me. He prunes every branch that bears fruit so that it will bear more fruit ... Remain in me, and I will remain in you. Just as the branch cannot bear fruit by itself, unless it remains in the vine, so neither can you unless you remain in me ... The one who remains in me – and I in him – bears much fruit, because apart from me you can accomplish nothing.

INSIGHT

Just as Jesus is the vine and his Father the gardener, we are the branches and Jesus is the vine. We have been uniquely created to stem out from Christ and to grow from him. Also notice here we are not striving to be the branches. Because of our position in Christ, we naturally become the branches of the true vine. It is a cause and effect, not from our own good deeds but because we choose to live in Christ. Again, Jesus shows us another representation of our adoption into a heavenly family.

PRAYER

Jesus, I pray my eyes would be set on you, that each day I would choose to rest in your presence. I pray that you will continue to grow in me the confidence of knowing my heavenly reflection. Thank you that you are my vine; thank you that I get all I need from you. I pray that just as the Father is trimming and pruning me, that I would do the same for myself. I pray that I, as part of the body, would grow into an integral piece of the heavenly vineyard, abundantly bearing all of the fruit of the Spirit. Overwhelm me each day, so much so that I could not stand a moment without you, that I would remain in you constantly, and you in me. Thank you, Lord, that the striving has ceased, that all I must do is seek your face. Thank you that you are the finisher and perfecter of my faith. To you be the glory forever and ever, amen.

DAY 12

ROMANS 5:1–2

Therefore, since we have been justified by faith, we have peace with God through our Lord Jesus Christ. Through him we have also obtained access by faith into this grace in which we stand, and we rejoice in hope of the glory of God.

INSIGHT

That we can be justified through faith is a beautiful gift. We no longer have to carry the impossible yoke of the Law. It is because of God's great love that he sent his Son for us! Through this one act of love, we have the freedom to live in his abundant grace. We can now rest in this grace, allowing God to prompt us through faith and hope into the things that display God's glory.

PRAYER

Thank you, Jesus, for becoming my spotless lamb.
It's because of you I can live by faith in God's
grace. I pray, Lord, that you would make me
sensitive to your Spirit, giving me ears to hear
your prompting. May everything I do be prompted
by faith, so that each day I am overwhelmed by
your glory. Thank you that I am no longer
burdened by carrying the yoke of the Law, but
instead I live freely in your grace. It is by your
grace I am saved. There is not one thing I could do
that could separate me from your love. I pray,
God, that as a result of your unconditional love, I
would love others as you love me. Show me how to
extend your heavenly grace to others so that I will
not be a person of judgment, but a person full of
forgiveness and love. May I always live for your
glory. I love and cherish you forever, amen.

DAY 13

MATTHEW 6:31–34

Therefore do not be anxious, saying, "What shall we eat?" or "What shall we drink?" or "What shall we wear?" For the Gentiles seek after all these things, and your heavenly Father knows that you need them all. But seek first the kingdom of God and his righteousness, and all these things will be added to you. Therefore do not be anxious about tomorrow, for tomorrow will be anxious for itself.

INSIGHT

God does not want us to be a people busy with planning out every move of our lives, nor does he desire us to live in fear of tomorrow. He longs to have us resting in his presence, waiting on him to direct us. I'm not saying we should sit and do nothing, rather we should first enjoy seeking him and then have him direct our steps. "For we walk by faith, not by sight" (2 Corinthians 5:7). We can look to the Word for many examples of walking by faith, whether it's about Noah, who was led by God to build an arch, or about Abraham's sacrifice of Isaac.

PRAYER

Lord, I pray and thank you that my heavenly position is established among heaven and earth. Thank you that I can rest in your presence and trust in your Spirit to guide my every move. Make me a person who truly knows how to walk by faith and not by sight. Lord, cause me to be a person who longs to seek you first. It's my heart's desire to fully trust you. Today, God, I am letting go; today I am laying aside my worries, my doubts, my fears. Today I reach my arms up to you, God; today I start my life afresh in your goodness, putting all things in your embrace. Thank you, Lord, for your steadfastness. I can always know that Papa is walking hand in hand with his beloved child. Increase in me love, increase in me faith, let me be a lamp on a hill shining your glory for all to see. I am your bride. I love and cherish you forever, amen.

DAY 14

ROMANS 6:6–11 (NET)

We know that our old man was crucified with him so that the body of sin would no longer dominate us, so that we would no longer be enslaved to sin. (For someone who has died has been freed from sin.) Now if we died with Christ, we believe that we will also live with him. We know that since Christ has been raised from the dead, he is never going to die again; death no longer has mastery over him. For the death he died, he died to sin once for all, but the life he lives, he lives to God. So you too consider yourselves dead to sin, but alive to God in Christ Jesus.

INSIGHT

Our old man has been crucified with him. How amazing is this? It's because of Jesus that we have died to sin and are alive through him! If we truly believe in this finished work of Christ—that we are now raised from spiritual death into an nonperishable life, then why would we ever put the yoke of sin back on? We should consider ourselves dead to sin, but alive to God in Christ Jesus!

PRAYER

Father, demolish any yoke of sin on my life and teach my heart how to live in the freedom of your beloved son, Jesus. Show my heart that upon accepting Jesus, the work was done. Just as Jesus died once to sin, so did I. Set my gaze fully on you, knowing that it's because of your goodness I can live in this beautiful freedom. As a result of your lovingkindness, I am made alive to you and dead to sin. Let me put my hand to the plow and never look back. I know that you have written my future, and you will always illuminate my path. Make my faith fresh today. Cause streams of living water to abundantly flow though my life. Shine your freedom through me like light calling in the lost and weary. You are the true God of grace and freedom. May the glory always be to you, forever and ever, amen!

DAY 15

JOHN 4:37–39

On the last day of the feast, the great day, Jesus stood up and cried out, "If anyone thirsts, let him come to me and drink. Whoever believes in me, as the Scripture has said, 'Out of his heart will flow rivers of living water.'" Now this he said about the Spirit, whom those who believed in him were to receive, for as yet the Spirit had not been given, because Jesus was not yet glorified.

INSIGHT

Jesus makes it so easy for us to be full of him. Notice that he doesn't say to first build a bucket, tie it to a rope, dig a well, then drink and be filled. No, he simply invites us to come and drink of him. All we must do is believe in him, and as a result we receive an abundance of living water! It is such an amazing gift that we do not have to do a laundry list of things to receive something as amazing as the Spirit.

PRAYER

Thank you, Papa, that you loved me with such an unfathomable love that you sent Jesus to be my bridegroom. Thank you that it's because of him I receive rivers of living water. I pray, Lord, that in my seeking of you through the Spirit, you will fill me full of living water to the point of total saturation. I pray that I am constantly thirsting for more of you, and I thank you that you will always quench this thirst. I pray that as you fill me, you will make me into a vessel that will carry living water to those who are also thirsty. Help me to pour out on those in need; help me to live in love. Cause me to be a person who constantly wants more of you. To you be the glory forever and ever, amen.

DAY 16

GALATIANS 2:19–21

For through the law I died to the law, so that I might live to God. I have been crucified with Christ. It is no longer I who live, but Christ who lives in me. And the life I now live in the flesh I live by faith in the Son of God, who loved me and gave himself for me. I do not nullify the grace of God, for if righteousness were through the law, then Christ died for no purpose.

INSIGHT

This is just another example of how we cannot be saved through our own works of righteousness. We should be comforted by this, because we do not have the burden of always tiptoeing through life, trying to be good enough. We can stand boldly before the throne knowing that Jesus stands as our advocate. We must learn how to accept this beautiful gift of grace and faithfully live in its promise. For if we deny what is given to us from the Father, we discredit the perfect gift of Jesus.

Prayer

Lord, I thank you for the gift of grace that freely
flows to me through the blood of Jesus. It is
because of this heavenly gift that I can live
peacefully in your presence. Cause all
stubbornness and any unbelief to be scattered into
oblivion. Draw me near to you by the Spirit that
lives in me, the Spirit that cries out *Abba Father.*
Remove from me any works of the Law so that my
soul's desire would not be for the Law but to live
in your goodness. Let me produce abundant fruit
as a result of your grace in my life. Perfect your
love in me, and help me to love others as Christ
loves me. You are the God of peace, the one who is
love. You are my Father, the one who lavishes
heavenly gifts upon me, his child. I give you praise
and honor forever, amen

DAY 17

PHILIPPIANS 4:10–14 (NET)

I have great joy in the Lord because now at last you have again expressed your concern for me ... I am not saying this because I am in need, for I have learned to be content in any circumstance. I have experienced times of need and times of abundance. In any and every circumstance I have learned the secret of contentment, whether I go satisfied or hungry, have plenty or nothing. I am able to do all things through the one who strengthens me. Nevertheless, you did well to share with me in my trouble

INSIGHT

I love that Paul is overwhelmed with joy, not because of what he can gain from people in a time of need, but because they have found a heart of love in brotherly affection. Paul is more satisfied knowing that Christ's love is being perfected in his fellow Christians than in meeting his own physical needs. He already knows that seeking Christ above all other things is what enables him to be content in any situation.

PRAYER

Lord, I pray that no matter what situation I face
in my life, I would look to you first, because you
are the one who satisfies all longing in my heart.
Show my heart, God, that you truly are the well
that will never run dry, that I can freely drink of
you and always be satisfied. Let not my concern
for my fellow Christians be set on what I can gain
from them, but that my heart would rejoice in
your love being perfected in their lives. Let not
one moment pass that I do not seek you first; that
no matter the situation, good or bad, I would look
to you. I pray that even in the darkest places, my
eyes would be fixed on the light only you provide.
In times of trouble, reveal to my heart the hope
and joy that comes from resting in life spent with
you. May my hands be lifted high to you forever
and ever, amen.

DAY 18

JOHN 14:12–14 (NET)

The person who believes in me will perform the miraculous deeds that I am doing, and will perform greater deeds than these, because I am going to the Father. And I will do whatever you ask in my name, so that the Father may be glorified in the Son. If you ask me anything in my name, I will do it.

INSIGHT

When we get insight and truth directly from Jesus, we really ought to listen! He was speaking to all who believed in his name while he was on earth. He is speaking to all of us who believe now! Why do we have such little faith then? Why do we hear of the things Jesus did but think we are not worthy of doing the same work? If we are truly a people that stands on God's Word, why can't we stand on this truth too? Jesus has gone to the Father to be our personal mediator and direct line to heaven. Let's be a people that stands boldly on this truth and go directly to the throne through the one who loves us—Christ Jesus.

PRAYER

Father, grow me in faith so that I would not be a person who shrinks away from your truth, but that stands in authority on your every word. Help my heart to see and understand your will for my life so that I would be a person who seeks you first. May I boldly step out in faith at every opportunity. Make me a person eager to heal the sick, and even raise the dead. I believe you have gone to the Father, and I know I have my direct line to heaven through you. May it never be about me, God. May every work in my life be a direct response to your love and guidance. Thank you for the boldness I can have when going before the throne. Thank you for making a way for me. To you be the honor and glory forever, amen.

DAY 19

MATTHEW 5:14–16

You are the light of the world. A city set on a hill cannot be hidden. Nor do people light a lamp and put it under a basket, but on a stand, and it gives light to all in the house. In the same way, let your light shine before others, so that they may see your good works and give glory to your Father who is in heaven.

INSIGHT

Now that we have put on Christ's righteousness, we are glowing and radiating in his glory. We must live out our lives in such a way that we are always bringing his light into a darkened world. "God is light, and in him is no darkness at all" (1 John 1:5). We must explore outwardly—from where we feel safe into darker territory, for we are the light.

Prayer

Lord, I pray your light would shine brighter than ever through me, that you would use me in all situations to bring your light into dark places. Thank you that you are the Father of light, that in you is no darkness. I pray, Father, that you would make me like a heavenly light on a hill, drawing in those who are lost and weary. Father, perfect your love in me that I would naturally walk as light at all times, never ceasing to bring you glory. Thank you for the privilege to bear your light. Thank you that angels surround my life and are singing heavenly songs. To you be the glory forever and ever, amen.

DAY 20

1 CORINTHIANS 13:1–3

If I speak in the tongues of men and of angels, but have not love, I am a noisy gong or a clanging cymbal. And if I have prophetic powers, and understand all mysteries and all knowledge, and if I have all faith, so as to remove mountains, but have not love, I am nothing. If I give away all I have, and if I deliver up my body to be burned, but have not love, I gain nothing.

INSIGHT

As we begin to rest in our heavenly reflection, we learn to no longer look to ourselves for validation. Christ living in us is what makes us perfect. It's at this point when God can truly start showing us how to love as he does. Love is God's highest command, and living in community with the Spirit enables us to live life out in true Christlike love. We can do all kinds of good works, but aside from being totally submissive to the Spirit and allowing our lives to be transformed into a representation of true fervent love, we are nothing! Today, break down the walls and rest in love.

PRAYER

Father, I pray that today I would see myself the way you see me. May I know I am free of all stains of unrighteousness because of Christ's blood flowing through my veins. I pray today, Papa, that your love would be perfected in me, that I would let go of trying to be good enough. I pray I would just rest in the love you have for me and be totally filled. Give me more opportunities to love. I know it's those strong in love who are called to carry the burdens of the weak. Show my heart that it's always love that leads to repentance, that I need not manage others' sin. Set me free from the burden of judgment and show me that I can trust you to judge fairly. Teach me that it's in this freedom from judgment that I can love freely. I pray you set loose in me a desire to love without boundaries!

DAY 21

ROMANS 8:37–39 (NET)

In all these things we have complete victory through him who loved us! ... neither death, nor life, nor angels, nor heavenly rulers, nor things that are present, nor things to come, nor powers, nor height, nor depth, nor anything else in creation will be able to separate us from the love of God in Christ Jesus our Lord.

INSIGHT

God has shown us perfect love, and we have complete victory through him! We don't have victory when we do enough good deeds or when we tithe more! Absolutely not! We have complete victory because our personal and loving God opened heavenly floodgates of love and grace to us, thanks to the blood of Jesus! Nothing can separate us from the love of God in Christ Jesus! No matter who is standing with sin or what people are doing in life, we can love them unconditionally. Is it said that we as a people are to be judges? Or rather, isn't it said that lovingkindness is what leads to repentance?

PRAYER

Papa, I pray that I sink into and rest in your love. Understanding your love and resting in your goodness causes me to be like you. Thank you, Papa, that because of Jesus, nothing can separate me from your love. Thank you that no matter where I am in life, you meet me there with open arms, ready to lavish affection on your child. Father, the way you love me can put a fire in me that will burn through all worldly thought. Your love resting in me can flow out streams of grace and mercy to those around me. I pray that this love would lead the world back to the one who is love, my God, the Father, the lord of love, and the perfecter of my faith. It is in this symphony of grace and love I have been called to dance! To you be the glory forever, amen.

DAY 22

GALATIANS 5:22–24

But the fruit of the Spirit is love, joy, peace, patience, kindness, goodness, faithfulness, gentleness, self-control; against such things there is no law. And those who belong to Christ Jesus have crucified the flesh with its passions and desires.

INSIGHT

The fruit is a direct reflection of Christ's character, and it's a magnificent thing to grasp the fullness of. It's only because of Jesus's death, burial, and resurrection that we have been given the ability to live life crucified to the flesh but alive to God through our adoption by the Spirit! Through the fruit of the Spirit, we know that all things are from God, and in this way we are confident that if we have any feelings creep into our lives that don't agree with the fruit, we know to crucify them, for they are not of God!

PRAYER

Father, I thank you for your Spirit, and that in him I have the ability to discern what is of you. I can know your will for my life. I pray, Papa, that your perfect love in me, through the total indwelling of the Spirit in my life, makes your desires become my own. I pray that I am truly and faithfully able to lay aside my own fleshly ambitions in exchange for your perfect plan for my life. Give me eyes of heaven so that I no longer see this world through the context of my flesh. Give me ears that hear only heavenly revelations. Papa, I pray for the strength to crucify all things of the flesh and to keep my eyes eternally focused on Jesus. Today, fill me with your Spirit; today, fill me with your love; today, let me bathe in your goodness. You are my dearly loved Father, the one who has called me his child. To you be my praise and honor forever, amen.

DAY 23

1 JOHN 4:9–12

By this the love of God is revealed in us: that God has sent his one and only Son into the world so that we may live through him. In this is love: not that we have loved God, but that he loved us and sent his Son to be the atoning sacrifice for our sins. Dear friends, if God so loved us, then we also ought to love one another.

INSIGHT

God is our perfect example of love. He loved us so much that he sent his son in the flesh to be our example of perfect love, through which we have been reconciled to sin and made alive to God! Through the sacrifice of Jesus, we can live alive to God through the Spirit, and through the Spirit we have the ability to love as Jesus did. If we allow the Spirit to love perfectly through us, we make heaven known on earth. We must allow the Spirit to move organically in our lives so that the end result is a love that supersedes all natural understanding. May we shine God's love and manifest heaven on earth through perfect love.

PRAYER

Papa, I pray that you would tear down all my walls of natural understanding when it comes to love. May you cause the Spirit to overcome all of my thoughts about what love is with your thoughts. Show me how to love as you love me. I pray, Father, and that the world would come to know you better as a result of this love. I believe that love perfected in the body shows others what heaven on earth looks like. Help me to lay aside all bitterness in my heart from judging others' sin. May I live life in the Spirit. To you be the glory, amen.

DAY 24

1 CORINTHIANS 12:12–13

For just as the body is one and has many members, and all the members of the body, though many, are one body, so it is with Christ. For in one Spirit we were all baptized into one body—Jews or Greeks, slaves or free—and all were made to drink of one Spirit.

INSIGHT

Through the baptism of the Spirit, we have all been made into one body in order to work together, in harmony, toward one common goal. In this unity we understand what it is to love one another more. The body cannot be divided if it is to be healthy. We must continue to encourage each other in our gifts, and to see heaven revealed on earth.

PRAYER

Father, I pray that I would be made sensitive to your Spirit, that you would cause me to live out my life in the body in perfect harmony. Let me not say I am not in need of others, for I know I am called to unite with others in one Spirit to work together for your will. Papa, cause your Spirit to fill me more each day so that my life would be fully consumed by your love. Let me truly know the worth of others, and may I understand that no one person is higher than another, but rather we are all placed perfectly by the one who is perfect. To you be the glory forever, amen.

DAY 25

2 CORINTHIANS 3:17–18 (NET)

Now the Lord is the Spirit, and where the Spirit of the Lord is present, there is freedom. And we all, with unveiled faces reflecting the glory of the Lord, are being transformed into the same image from one degree of glory to another.

INSIGHT

God knows us and loves us so much that he sent Jesus to bring a new covenant, a better covenant—one of freedom, love, and grace. We now have the honor of removing the veil that was once laid over our faces, and we see God directly through his Spirit. God's glory is reflecting out of us by allowing the Spirit to move in our lives. Just as Paul once said "But by the grace of God I am what I am" (1 Corinthians 15:10), so should we be at peace with our righteousness and stop striving to be holy. We can simply let go and let God take over. This is God's will for our lives—to be in relationship with a good daddy and let him bring us from glory to glory.

PRAYER

Thank you, Papa, that the veil has been removed and that I can have a personal relationship with you through your Spirit. Thank you that you are guiding me each day, that you are holding my hand as I walk through life like the good Father you are. I thank you so much, Daddy, that you have a plan and a purpose for me. All I must do is seek you. I pray that I would be in a constant state of letting go and that you would influence every aspect of my life. I pray that I could look at my life and stand firmly in the same truth Paul states (that by the grace of God he is what he is), and live in the confidence of the Spirit. I, too, am being brought into your radiant glory, and I am living life in the Spirit in such a way that I can only boast of your goodness. To you be the glory forever, amen.

DAY 26

EPHESIANS 1:3–6

Who has blessed us in Christ with every spiritual blessing in the heavenly places, even as he chose us in him before the foundation of the world, that we should be holy and blameless before him. In love he predestined for adoption to himself as sons through Jesus Christ, according to the purpose of his will.

INSIGHT

God is holding nothing back from us. He is lavishing on us every spiritual blessing that is in the heavenly realms! God has specifically chosen each one of us, before the foundation of the earth, to be blameless and holy before him in perfect love. We have been predestined to be sons and daughters for specific purposes. This is how special and loved we are! If we have been given these promises, we can look through all circumstances and straight to the cross. If we set our sights on Jesus, all else will crumble away, and we will live according to Papa's purpose for our lives by our Spirit.

PRAYER

Papa, thank you that you're not holding anything back from me, but rather you pour out all that is heavenly on me in a symphony of grace. Thank you for giving me a heavenly purpose on earth so that my life would have great meaning. I pray, Papa, your love for me would be made more known than ever so I would never be able to step into shame or fear again. Father, cause my heart to only look to you, knowing that each day I can bring heaven to earth. I pray that your love for me would cause my eyes to always be set on Jesus, that each day I would carry out your will in perfect love for others. To you be the glory forever, amen.

DAY 27

EPHESIANS 1:7–10

In him we have redemption through his blood, the forgiveness of our trespasses, according to the riches of his grace, which he lavished upon us, in all wisdom and insight making known to us the mystery of his will, according to his purpose, which he set forth in Christ as a plan for the fullness of time, to unite all things in him, things in heaven and things on earth.

INSIGHT

By his grace we are made completely righteous before God the Father. Through Jesus, he lavishes wisdom and insight on us, and he makes known the mystery of his will. It is only because of Jesus that we can live a life in the Spirit, one full of purpose and promise. We have all been called in love to unite all things to Christ, both on earth and in heaven, in one Spirit. So come, church: let us together, in one Spirit, unite in our heavenly purpose—to see our Father's will be done on earth as it is in heaven.

PRAYER

I pray, Papa, that today you would make known my heavenly position. May I be overcome by your presence. I ask that each day you would direct me in your will, because I know you are using me even now to bring heaven to earth. I pray, Papa, that you would tear down all my preconceived notions of love and build a foundation of perfect love that's from heaven. Help me to always walk boldly beside you, and that your Spirit would always fall on me like heavenly robes. Thank you for your amazing love toward me. To you be the glory forever, amen.

DAY 28

EPHESIANS 4:21–24

Assuming that you have heard about him and were taught in him, as the truth is in Jesus, to put off your old self, which belongs to your former manner of life and is corrupt through deceitful desires, and to be renewed in the spirit of your minds, and to put on the new self, created after the likeness of God in true righteousness and holiness.

INSIGHT

Through our adoption into a heavenly family, we have been taught in him, who is Jesus. We now have the gift of the Spirit, and through the Spirit we are able to put on our new person. This new person is a direct reflection of heaven. We must stand firmly in this new position, understanding we have been made holy through the one who loves us. Let the Spirit constantly and continuously transform us into the righteous and holy image of Christ.

PRAYER

Father, I pray that today you would help me put
aside the old man and trust in you. I know I have
entered a relationship with you, and I can have
constant fellowship with you through the Spirit. I
pray that today you would renew me even more in
your Spirit, and I would step completely into my
new self. May I never look back to the old self but
constantly fix my eyes on my heavenly reflection.
May I be confident and know that it is all finished,
that Jesus already paid the price. Let me live out
the rest of my life in true righteousness and
holiness, loving everyone because you have loved
all. To you always be the glory, amen.

DAY 29

EPHESIANS 6:10–13 (NET)

Finally, be strengthened in the Lord and in the strength of his power. Clothe yourselves with the full armor of God so that you may be able to stand against the schemes of the devil. For our struggle is not against flesh and blood, but against the rulers, against the powers, against the world rulers of this darkness, against the spiritual forces of evil in the heavens. For this reason, take up the full armor of God so that you may be able to stand your ground on the evil day, and having done everything, to stand.

INSIGHT

While being strengthened in Christ and living life in our heavenly reflection, we must also equip ourselves in all that God gives us. He has given us armor to put on, and we are to wear it confidently as we engage what is not seen. There is a conflict happening as we speak, but God, in his great love, has equipped us in every way to stand firm in our faith. Let us today put on his full armor and be a people united in bringing heaven to earth!

PRAYER

Papa, I pray that today you would fasten every buckle of my spiritual armor. May my shield of faith be unbreakable, and may my sword be sharpened so as to cut through any scheme of the devil. Thank you that I can stand firmly on the foundation you built for me, and that the building's cornerstone is Christ Jesus. I pray that you would give me eyes to see and ears to hear that which otherwise is unseen. Unite me with others today to be a person who functions as part of one body to bring your glory to the earth. To you be the glory forever, amen.

DAY 30

EPHESIANS 3:16–18 (NET)

Be strengthened with power through his Spirit in the inner person, that Christ may dwell in your hearts through faith, so that, because you have been rooted and grounded in love, you may be able to comprehend with all the saints what is the breadth and length and height and depth, and thus to know the love of Christ that surpasses knowledge, so that you may be filled up to all the fullness of God.

INSIGHT

Through faith we invite the Spirit to dwell in our hearts. It is because of the Spirit we can truly fulfill a life rooted in love. Though we were once people of the world, we are now transformed into the image of God. We have been given a new identity in Christ; we are now living as his heavenly reflection, radiating his glory on the earth. It's in this perfect relationship that we can begin to understand the vastness of his love for us. We must break down all the walls of religion and simply live life loving and seeking Jesus.

PRAYER

Papa, I pray for confidence to live life in my true reflection of heaven—no longer seeing myself but the reflection of Jesus living in me. Thank you for tearing down religion and bringing me into a new covenant, a better covenant, one that's built on a foundation of love. I pray that through my faith, I would be brought closer to you, and that each day I would have new opportunities to bring your kingdom to earth. Thank you for your endless grace and your constant pursuit of your bride. To you always be the glory, amen.

DAY 31

(for months with that extra day)

THE BUTTERFLY EFFECT OF LIVING A SPIRIT-FILLED LIFE

The journey of coming to know Christ can be like the life journey of a butterfly. We start out born into life as a rather silly little grub, inching around life in a crude fashion. This is sufficient for some time, for we are living and surviving. As we mature into the adult caterpillar, this redundant life we've been living just doesn't cut it anymore. We begin to realize there's more to life than merely inching around and scrounging for our next meal. We know there is something more, something bigger. There is a destiny for us, one we don't quite understand yet.

Then it happens: one day we let go of merely striving to get by and we grab hold of hope. This hope is in Christ, the one who transforms us into his likeness. Before you know it, we find ourselves in a cocoon of love, trust, grace, and mercy. There is a beautiful and natural process happening within our hearts. We are indeed going to emerge as a new creation. When that day comes, we emerge more beautiful than we could have ever dreamed. We went from ugly hairy grubs inching around to this magnificent display of glory.

As we break free from our cocoons for the first time, our wings stretch to the heavens, glimmering in vibrant colors of glory and wonder. While still uncertain of our ability to fly, a breeze from heaven sweeps under us, lifting us to flight. Now soaring on grace, our transformation is made real. Now we understand who we are; now we understand our purpose.

As we soar on wings made new, a sweet aroma tugs at our senses. As we fly nearer to the garden, we see the glory of the flowers of the field. Just like moth to flame, we are drawn to them with an uncontrollable passion. We drink of the flowers' nectar, we eat of their pollen until we become completely satisfied. The flowers represent Christ, because we are fully satisfied when filling ourselves with him.

Our lives are not merely this as butterflies; we must go field to field in a display of God's glory, spreading the pollen of life from one garden to the next. We fill ourselves so as to pour out on the next garden, so as to ensure the harvest is plentiful. Dusty, once bare fields become lush and abundant. In this we have been made into a new creation, and we've realized our potential.

Just as the butterflies originated from caterpillars, we, too, in our lives on earth, have stepped out of our old selves and put on the radiant glory of Christ. We then must also fill ourselves with his goodness and pollinate the fields of the earth with his love.

ABOUT THE AUTHOR

Shawn Thompson was born in a small mountain town near Colorado Springs, Colorado. Most of his life, he never wanted anything to do with God ... until one day God encountered him and changed the trajectory of his life forever. Ever since this profound experience with God, Shawn has been searching in the deepest parts of the Father's heart and revealing the Father's love to a world that has lost its heavenly identity. It is Shawn's true passion to show the world that the God of history is not a god of judgment and wrath, but a Father who desires a loving relationship with all of his children.

CONTACT SHAWN

WEBSITE: paradiseunlocked.com

INSTAGRAM: @paradise_unlocked

FACEBOOK: facebook.com/paradiseunlockedmaui

E-MAIL: shawnwthompson@icloud.com

www.ingramcontent.com/pod-product-compliance
Lightning Source LLC
Chambersburg PA
CBHW061156040426
42445CB00013B/1705